Original title:
The Secret Valley

Copyright © 2024 Creative Arts Management OÜ
All rights reserved.

Author: Cameron Blair
ISBN HARDBACK: 978-9916-90-806-8
ISBN PAPERBACK: 978-9916-90-807-5

Serenade of the Muffled Stream

A gentle flow beneath the boughs,
Whispers soft of nature's vows.
Rippling tunes, a hidden rhyme,
Dancing echoes through the time.

Pebbles glisten, water's grace,
In corners cool, a secret place.
Rustling leaves, a soft refrain,
Shimmering notes in gentle rain.

Secrets Cradled by the Hills

Silent whispers reach the sky,
Hills embrace where dreams comply.
Softly swaying, shadows blend,
Nature's tales that never end.

Among the trees, the whispers sigh,
Ancient secrets, soft and shy.
In twilight's glow, stories weave,
Heartfelt tales, we believe.

Footprints of the Unknown Garden

Paths untraveled, soft and bright,
Hidden blooms in morning light.
With each step, curiosities rise,
A world untouched, before our eyes.

Petals flutter, secrets call,
In this haven, spirits enthrall.
Whispers linger, dreams take flight,
In garden's heart, day meets night.

Echoes in the Private Clearing

Whispers carried on the breeze,
Silence lingers 'neath the trees.
Footsteps fade, yet still they stay,
Memories dance in soft array.

Stars awaken in the dusk,
Mysteries wrapped in evening's husk.
In this space, where hearts lay bare,
Time stands still, and dreams can share.

Illuminations in the Shade

Under the branches, whispers play,
Sunlight dances, golden ray.
Shadows linger, secrets confined,
In the stillness, solace you'll find.

Petals drift through twilight's sigh,
Silent moments, as dreams pass by.
Nature's canvas, soft and wide,
In the shade, let your heart reside.

Veils of the Forgotten Seasons

In the breeze, old tales unfold,
Whispers of time, echoes bold.
Frosted leaves and sunlit skies,
Memories linger, never die.

Autumn's cloak, a fading hue,
Winter's breath, a chilling dew.
Through each veil, we journey on,
In forgotten seasons, life goes on.

Embrace of the Uncharted Refuge

Nestled deep where wild things roam,
In the heart of the unknown home.
Nature calls with a gentle song,
In her arms, where we belong.

Stars above in a velvet sky,
Guiding paths where the dreamers fly.
In the refuge, fears set free,
Embraced by all that's meant to be.

Solstice in the Enclosed Green

Beneath the sun, the world awakes,
In the green, a heartbeat shakes.
Leaves are dancing, spirits rise,
In the warmth, the future lies.

Time stands still where shadows merge,
In this green, we feel the surge.
Solstice moments, bright and keen,
Life's embrace in the enclosed green.

Beneath the Canopy of Secrets

Whispers dance on the gentle breeze,
Old trees guard their mysteries.
Shadows play where sunlight weaves,
In this realm, all time believes.

Rustling leaves tell tales untold,
Of dreams and wishes, brave and bold.
Creatures lurking, spirits keen,
In nature's heart, they glide unseen.

Twilight in the Concealed Glade

Fading light in the quiet woods,
Colors blend like muted hoods.
Fireflies twinkle in soft ballet,
Nature's voice begins to sway.

Moonlight dances on silver streams,
Reflecting softly on hidden dreams.
Silence whispers through the air,
Secrets linger everywhere.

The Trail to the Enigma

Footsteps crunch on the worn-out ground,
Echoes linger, a haunting sound.
Every turn, a new surprise,
Curious paths disguise the lies.

Mossy stones lead to unknown lore,
Each stride whispers what came before.
With every heartbeat, mysteries draw,
Tales entwined, forever in awe.

Secrets of the Undiscovered Dell

Hidden deep where shadows lie,
Softened hush beneath the sky.
Nature's bounty, lush and green,
Holds the beauty yet unseen.

A brook hums low with gentle tunes,
Past secrets bound in croons and runes.
A world untouched, a sacred space,
In the dell, we find our place.

Solitude of the Enshrouded Hollows

In the hollowed depths, shadows weave,
A stillness thick, that few perceive.
Whispers linger, secrets grow,
In the quiet, time moves slow.

Roots entwine in earth's embrace,
Forgotten life, a hidden space.
Echoes of a world once bright,
Drift away in fading light.

Mossy stones hold stories grim,
Where spirits dance on nature's whim.
A solitude that breathes and sighs,
Beneath the vast, unending skies.

The Tapestry of Untold Stories

Each thread a tale, spun through the years,
Woven with laughter, stitched with tears.
Colors vivid, shades so bright,
A tapestry wrapped in soft twilight.

In corners hidden, dreams take flight,
In every stitch, a memory's light.
Fables whispered, journeys traced,
Lives entwined and time embraced.

Patterns shift, new paths unfold,
Past and future, rich and bold.
In the fabric, hearts remain,
Silent echoes, love and pain.

Murmurs under the Twilit Canopy

Beneath the boughs where shadows play,
Murmurs of night begin their sway.
A gentle rustle, leaves softly sigh,
Secrets shared where the dark birds fly.

Stars blink above, a twinkling span,
The hush of dusk, a tranquil plan.
Crickets serenade the fading light,
Softly calling through the night.

In this realm where dreams arise,
Whispers dance like fireflies.
Underneath the twilight's grace,
Find solace in this sacred space.

The Grotto of Lost Dreams

In the grotto deep, where shadows dwell,
Echoes linger, a haunting bell.
Dreams once bright now softly fade,
In the stillness, hope displayed.

Starlit mists weave through the night,
A shimmering veil, a ghostly sight.
Fragments of wishes, half-shed tears,
Hide within, lost through the years.

Waves of silence, a soothing balm,
In this refuge, a fragile calm.
Among the stones, life's tales rewind,
In the grotto, peace we find.

Lurking Beauty of the Invisible

In shadows deep where whispers sigh,
Petals hide, and secrets lie.
A dance of forms in twilight's glow,
Nurtured dreams the night may show.

Cloaked in mist, their grace concealed,
The heart of longing remains unsealed.
An echo twirls, a wisp in flight,
Enticing souls in fading light.

Soliloquy of the Obscured Garden

Among the leaves where silence weaves,
A story rests, no one believes.
Fragments of time in whispers pass,
The bloom of memory in the grass.

Creeping vines in tangled scheme,
Veil the truths that once did gleam.
Soft petals speak in language rare,
Secrets woven with utmost care.

Songs from the Cloistered Glen

In shaded nooks where shadows blend,
A melody begins to trend.
Notes like drops of morning dew,
Whisper tales both old and new.

Each breeze, a symphony of grace,
Carrying dreams from place to place.
Harmony drips from every tree,
In this secluded reverie.

The Allure of the Silent Vale

Beneath the surface, still and deep,
A world awakens from its sleep.
Gentle whispers call the brave,
To seek the solace of the wave.

Shadows merge with twilight's reign,
Cascades of silence cleanse the pain.
Here the heart finds solace, true,
In the vale where dreams renew.

Heartstrings of the Concealed Realm

In shadows deep where whispers dwell,
The heartstrings pull, a silent spell.
Through hidden paths, old stories weave,
In secret corners, hopes deceive.

With echoes soft, the whispers play,
A dance of dreams at end of day.
The concealed realm beckons near,
As secrets bloom, the heart can hear.

The Gardener of Hidden Secrets

In twilight hours, the gardener waits,
With tender hands, he cultivates fates.
Amongst the weeds, the stories grow,
In silent soil, truths start to show.

The flowers bloom with colors rare,
Each petal holds a whispered care.
In shadows cast by moonlit beams,
The gardener tends to silent dreams.

Celestial Whispers in the Thicket

Beneath the stars, a thicket stirs,
Whispers dance like gentle furs.
Each leaf a word, each sound a sigh,
In celestial tales, the spirits fly.

The night unfolds its velvet cloak,
While voices blend in sacred folk.
With every rustle, secrets split,
In that stillness, hearts submit.

The Moonlit Portal of Secrets

A portal shines with silver light,
Its secrets held till cloaks of night.
With cautious steps, we walk the way,
As shadows greet the dawning day.

In moonlight's glow, the past awakes,
Unveiling truths in quiet lakes.
Through whispered words, we find the key,
To unlock dreams in mystery.

The Myth of the Enclosed Vale

In the vale where whispers play,
Legends sleep, and shadows sway.
Time stands still, a gentle sigh,
Beneath the vast, unending sky.

Here the dawn brings secrets bright,
Shimmering with the morning light.
Echoes of the tales we've spun,
Fade like mist when day is done.

Ancient trees weave stories old,
Of dreams that wander, brave and bold.
In the silence, hearts can feel,
The enchantment of the concealed.

Yet as the stars begin to bloom,
History stirs from tender gloom.
The vale holds close its sacred lore,
A myth that lives forevermore.

Journey Through the Concealed Woodlands

Through the woods where shadows dance,
Footsteps echo, a fleeting chance.
Leafy canopies above us sway,
Guiding us on our winding way.

Beneath the arches, secrets hide,
Whispers carried by the tide.
Nature paints with vibrant hues,
Each turn reveals a tale to choose.

Misty paths adorned with dew,
Lead us to realms both strange and true.
In this haven of verdant grace,
We find our heart, our sacred space.

Amidst the ferns, a tranquil peace,
In the woods, our worries cease.
With every step, the world fades fast,
As we spellbind in nature's cast.

Reverence of the Hidden Enclave

In the enclave where silence reigns,
Time embraces, soft refrains.
Whispers float on tranquil air,
With every breath, a moment rare.

Ancient stones and mossy ground,
Nature's art in echoes found.
Here, the heart learns how to pause,
In the stillness, find its cause.

Sunlight filters through the leaves,
Each beam a thread that gently weaves.
In this refuge from the noise,
We discover life's hidden joys.

With reverence, we bow and kneel,
To forces felt but never revealed.
In the sanctuary of the soul,
The enclave whispers, making us whole.

Secrets Wrapped in Emerald Leaves

In the green where secrets lay,
Emerald leaves cradle the day.
Underneath the boughs so wide,
Whispers of old dreams abide.

Nature's clasp holds stories tight,
In the shadows, they find light.
Each leaf a page, each root a tale,
Of wanderers who dared to sail.

Muffled truths in the forest's heart,
Inviting souls to come and part.
Through the rustle, we hear the call,
Of ancient wisdom shared with all.

Secrets bloom in the fading sun,
In the leaves, our spirits run.
Through emerald depths, we come to see,
The world's magic, wild and free.

Veins of Life in the Secreted Terrain

In shadows deep where whispers dwell,
Roots entwine, a sacred spell.
Beneath the earth, secrets betide,
Veins of life where dreams reside.

All around, the earth does sigh,
Leaves converse beneath the sky.
In crumbled paths, the stories weave,
Tales of those who dared believe.

Sunlight dances on the ground,
Nature's pulse, a steady sound.
In the soil, the ancient ties,
Connect the past where silence lies.

In hidden realms, the heartbeats flow,
Life emerges, soft and slow.
With every stir, the world expands,
Veins of life in unseen hands.

Ciphers in the Emerald Shadows

In emerald glades where secrets hide,
Ciphers twist, the heart will bide.
Branches sway with words unspoken,
Nature's code, a bond unbroken.

Whispers echo through the leaves,
Meaning thrums in what deceives.
Patterns swirl in sunlight's gleam,
Silent messages in a dream.

Shadows dance, a fleeting grace,
Telling stories in a trace.
Hidden truths in colors bright,
Ciphers glow in fading light.

Beneath the boughs, the spell is cast,
The forest speaks of ages past.
Each glance reveals a world anew,
Emerald shadows, wisdom true.

History Buried in Leafy Embrace

In leafy beds, the past is laid,
Whispers of ancients softly played.
Forgotten tales in rustling green,
History's echo, softly seen.

Roots extend with stories grim,
Through branches high, the light grows dim.
Nature guards each fleeting age,
In silent books of earth and sage.

With every gust, the leaves do sigh,
Recalling when the world was shy.
Beneath the canopy, time stands still,
In leafy embrace, we feel the thrill.

Moments etched where no one goes,
In sepulchral paths, the wisdom flows.
Guardians of tales forever remain,
History buried in leafy reign.

A Lullaby of Forgotten Echoes

In twilight's grasp, the echoes weave,
A lullaby for hearts that grieve.
Softly sung in dusky light,
Melodies of the fading night.

Chants of old from yonder day,
Whisper through as shadows play.
Lost in time, the songs emerge,
From depths where silent dreams surge.

The wind carries their tender tune,
Beneath the watchful, blankened moon.
Each note a kiss, a gentle sigh,
In the dark where memories lie.

So hush your heart, let silence be,
Embrace the night, set your soul free.
In forgotten echoes, you'll find peace,
A lullaby that will never cease.

Shimmers in the Dappled Light

Through the leaves, sunlight plays,
Creating patterns in soft shades.
Whispers dance on gentle breeze,
Nature's art in silent ease.

Flowers bloom in vibrant hues,
As the day begins to muse.
Golden rays touch tender ground,
In this peace, my heart is found.

Under branches, shadows creep,
Secrets that the forest keeps.
Magic glows where heartbeats meet,
In this realm, I feel complete.

Every moment is a song,
In the light where I belong.
Captured in this tranquil sight,
Life's soft shimmers, pure delight.

The Lost Realm of Shadows

In the twilight, whispers call,
Echoes through the ancient hall.
Forgotten paths where silence weeps,
Beneath the stars, the secret keeps.

Veils of mystery enfold the night,
Guided only by the pale starlight.
Figures dance in muted grace,
In this realm, time leaves no trace.

A shroud of dreams, a silent song,
Where lost souls wander, still and long.
In shadows deep, their stories blend,
A haunting tale that knows no end.

Here in darkness, truth unveils,
Beyond the light, the spirit sails.
Through the mist, the lost souls roam,
In shadows deep, they find their home.

Trails of the Veiled Wanderer

Along the path where shadows weave,
The wanderer's heart takes its leave.
Hidden trails beneath the boughs,
Secrets whispered with the vows.

Footsteps soft on mossy ground,
In silence, stories yet unfound.
Each corner turned, a new surprise,
The world unfolds before my eyes.

Beneath the stars, a guiding hint,
Trailing light where shadows print.
With every step, I leave behind,
The echoes of a restless mind.

In the night, the whispers swell,
A tale of journeys yet to tell.
Through the veil, my spirit flies,
On trails where only silence lies.

Solitude in the Silent Thicket

In the stillness, peace I find,
Nature's touch, a gentle bind.
Amidst the thicket, quiet reigns,
In solitude, the spirit gains.

Leaves like whispers brush my cheek,
In this silence, I can speak.
Thoughts like rivers, softly flow,
In nature's arms, I softly grow.

The world outside fades away,
In this thicket, I long to stay.
Moments linger, time stands still,
In solitude, I find my will.

Here, beneath the leafy dome,
I discover the heart of home.
In this quiet, life takes flight,
Solitude in the silent night.

Whispers of the Hidden Glade

In shadows deep, the secrets lie,
Where soft winds sigh, and spirits fly,
Among the ferns, the silence sings,
In whispered tones, the forest clings.

A glade adorned with emerald shades,
Where time stands still, and peace invades,
The fluttering leaves, a gentle dance,
Invite the heart to take a chance.

Each step reveals a world anew,
With sunlit paths and skies of blue,
The hidden glade, a sacred space,
Where nature's breath finds its embrace.

So linger here, in quiet grace,
And let your soul this stillness taste,
For in the whispers, wisdom grows,
In hidden glades, the spirit flows.

Enchantment Among Forgotten Hills

The hills arise, a timeless lot,
Where echoes dwell, and dreams are caught,
In twilight's glow, the magic stirs,
A symphony of silent purrs.

Among the stones, the stories weave,
Of ancient paths and what they leave,
The wind carries tales of old,
In whispered lore, they brave and bold.

Each step unveils a mystery,
In shadows deep, the wild is free,
The moon alights the pathways clear,
As nature dances near and dear.

In this enchantment, hearts will soar,
Among the hills, forevermore,
For those who wander, dreams unfold,
In whispered grace, their spirits hold.

Echoes of a Mystic Grove

In mystic groves where shadows play,
The echoes call, night meets the day,
Among the trees, a secret song,
That lures the heart to dance along.

Each rustling leaf, a soft refrain,
In harmony with nature's gain,
The twilight whispers, soft and low,
In ancient rhythms, tides do flow.

With every step upon the ground,
The pulse of life is deeply found,
In sacred circles, spirits meet,
In quiet places, time's retreat.

Embrace the echoes, let them guide,
Through moonlit paths where dreams abide,
In the grove's embrace, find your way,
Where echoes linger and softly sway.

Beneath the Canopy of Dreams

Beneath the canopy, stars gleam bright,
A world awakens in the soft night,
Whispers of hope in the cool, crisp air,
As dreams take flight without a care.

Among the branches, the nightingale sings,
Stories of love and all it brings,
The gentle rustle of leaves above,
Cradling the heart in rhythms of love.

Here every shadow has a grace,
A tale to tell, a sacred place,
With every breath, the magic flows,
In stillness found, the spirit knows.

So wander freely, let worries cease,
Beneath the dreams, embrace the peace,
For in the night, the stars will gleam,
In hidden realms, we find the dream.

The Solace of Unseen Meadows

In fields where daisies softly sway,
The whispers of the breeze hold sway.
Each petal opens, secrets unfold,
In silent tales, nature's gold.

Beneath the vast, cerulean sky,
The days drift like clouds passing by.
With every rustle, a gentle sigh,
Time is a friend that cannot lie.

In the hush of dusk, shadows blend,
A symphony where all hearts mend.
With twilight's brush, the colors fade,
Yet memories of joy never jade.

So here I'll sit, in bliss embraced,
In unseen meadows, peace interlaced.
A moment caught, a life well spent,
In nature's lap, my heart's content.

Tales from the Obscured Pastures

Beneath the hills where silence reigns,
Stories linger like soft, sweet chains.
In every blade, a voice can speak,
Of ancient times and futures sleek.

Amidst the trees, shadows conspire,
To weave the tales that never tire.
With whispers soft, the winds narrate,
Of lovers lost and twisted fate.

The stars above twinkle and grin,
As if they know what lies within.
From dashed hopes to dreams reborn,
In the pastures where souls are worn.

Each step we take, a path unfolds,
In obscured meadows, secrets hold.
So come, dear friend, let's forge our creed,
In these pastures, where we are freed.

Sanctuary Among Starlit Ferns

In the quiet of night, magic brews,
Where starlight dances with dew-kissed views.
Among the ferns, shadows take flight,
A sanctuary in the heart of night.

The soft rustle of leaves whispers low,
Inviting the moon to join the show.
With every flicker and every sigh,
The beauty of dusk makes spirits fly.

Here dreams are woven in silken threads,
In the embrace of the earth's soft beds.
Where worries fade with the setting sun,
A tranquil realm where all is one.

So let us linger among the ferns,
In this sanctuary, my heart yearns.
With stars above as our steadfast guide,
In nature's arms, let love abide.

The Dance of Elusive Fireflies

In twilight's glow, a spark ignites,
The dance of fireflies in warm, soft nights.
They flicker and weave in a playful trance,
Painting the air with a glowing dance.

Each light a story, a dream to share,
While shadows deepen, we breathe the air.
With laughter echoing in the breeze,
We chase the lights 'neath the whispering trees.

The world slows down, as if to hear,
The songs of the night, so crystal clear.
In this enchanted, fleeting show,
We find a joy that starts to grow.

So follow the lights, let your heart sway,
In the dance of fireflies, come what may.
For in their glow, we find delight,
A timeless moment, pure and bright.

The Hidden Oasis

In the heart of the sands, it lies,
With waters that glisten, under the skies.
Palm trees sway, secrets they keep,
Guarding dreams in shadows deep.

A breeze whispers tales of old,
Of wanderers brave and treasures bold.
The sun dips low, painting the land,
In hues of gold, a beauty so grand.

Ripples dance, reflecting light,
As the stars awaken in the night.
Crickets sing a soothing tune,
Beneath the watchful, glowing moon.

Here time stands still, in pure delight,
Each moment savored, deep and bright.
The hidden oasis, a retreat divine,
A sanctuary where hearts align.

Voices from the Silent Grove

In the grove where silence reigns,
Whispers of the past, like gentle rains.
Leaves rustle softly, secrets unfold,
Stories etched in bark, waiting to be told.

The paths are woven with dreams and time,
Each step echoes a forgotten rhyme.
Moss carpets the ground, a lush embrace,
Nature's quiet essence fills the space.

Juvenile birds take flight in glee,
Vivid hues against the ancient tree.
A creek flows softly, crystal clear,
Murmurs of wisdom for those who hear.

In stillness, the world fades away,
Only the grove and its voices stay.
Here in the hush, the soul can roam,
Finding solace, a true sense of home.

Enigma of the Cloistered Thicket

Deep within the ancient wood,
Where shadows linger, still and good.
A thicket cloaked in mystery's hue,
With tales of wonder, known to few.

Branches twist, like thoughts entwined,
Guarding secrets, a heart aligned.
Flashes of light through leaves dapple,
Encouraging the soul to grapple.

Elusive paths that twist and turn,
In every thicket, lessons learn.
The rustle of creatures, a soft serenade,
In the fog of day, wonder displayed.

Moments captured in quiet grace,
Each heartbeat echoes in this space.
The thicket's enigma, a soft embrace,
Inviting souls to seek their place.

Beneath the Whispering Boughs

Beneath the boughs where silence sings,
Dreams take flight on hidden wings.
Dappled sunlight, a golden lace,
Wraps the earth in a warm embrace.

Gentle breezes carry a tune,
From dawn's blush to the rise of the moon.
A harmony found in the rustling leaves,
Where every heartache softly grieves.

The world outside fades, a distant call,
In this sanctuary, serenity enthralls.
Time ticks slow in this verdant space,
Each moment lingers, a sweet trace.

Under the sky, vast and wide,
Life's mysteries are bared, not denied.
Beneath the whispering boughs, truth flows,
In the quiet depths, the spirit grows.

Secrets of the Fern-Filled Hollow

Amidst the shadows green and deep,
The whispers of the ferns do creep.
In twilight's glow, a dance they weave,
Unraveling tales that few believe.

Each frond a keeper of the past,
In silence, secrets hold them fast.
A realm where time does softly bend,
And nature's wonders never end.

The brook sings low, a gentle hum,
While nightfall's cloak brings dreams that come.
In every rustle, life takes flight,
In fern-filled hollow, pure delight.

With every step, a soft embrace,
A hidden haven, sacred space.
In silence shared, we find our place,
The fern-filled hollow, nature's grace.

Nature's Veil: A Hidden Paradise

Beneath the boughs, where shadows play,
A hidden paradise does sway.
In dappled light, the leaves converse,
A symphony, beautiful and terse.

The flowers bloom in secret hues,
With fragrant whispers, they infuse.
The breeze carries a soothing song,
In nature's realm, where we belong.

Each step unveils a world anew,
With every glance, a vibrant view.
The streams that sing and rocks that gleam,
A magic woven, like a dream.

This veiled escape, where hearts can heal,
In nature's arms, we learn to feel.
A hidden paradise, our retreat,
Where every moment feels complete.

The Allure of Uncharted Wilds

Beyond the path, where few have tread,
The wilds call out, our fears we shed.
Uncharted lands stretch far and wide,
In nature's arms, we run, we hide.

A tapestry of green and gold,
Each story of adventure told.
With every turn, a new surprise,
In secret valleys, under skies.

The mountains rise, so strong, so vast,
Reminders of a shadowed past.
In wild terrains, the spirits soar,
An allure that beckons evermore.

Through tangled woods and rivers' flow,
The heart ignites, the spirit glows.
In uncharted wilds, we find our way,
In nature's beauty, we long to stay.

Laughter of the Hidden Springs

Where silence met the gurgling streams,
The water dances, laughter beams.
In hidden glades, the echoes play,
A joyous tune that leads the way.

With every splash, a sparkle bright,
The springs reveal their pure delight.
Amongst the stones, the whispers flow,
In nature's grasp, the heart does glow.

The laughter rings from every bend,
In moments shared, we start to mend.
Beneath the sun, the world feels right,
In hidden springs, our spirits light.

We gather by the water's edge,
United in our simple pledge.
To cherish laughs, the joy it brings,
To live as one with hidden springs.

Beneath the Starlit Veil

Whispers float on gentle breeze,
Underneath the ancient trees.
Stars align in twinkling song,
Guiding hearts where they belong.

Moonlight dances on the ground,
Casting shadows all around.
Dreams unfold in silver light,
As the world fades from our sight.

Night unfolds her velvet cloak,
In stillness, secrets softly spoke.
Beneath this vast and open sky,
Hope and wonder drift on high.

Together, lost in reverie,
Beneath the starlit canopy.
We'll find our way where dreams may dwell,
In the magic of night's sweet spell.

Retreat of the Dreamer's Spirit

In twilight's embrace, we gather near,
A sanctuary free from fear.
Floating thoughts in gentle hues,
Whisper tales of endless muse.

The world outside begins to fade,
As peaceful moments serenade.
Within this place, our spirits soar,
A refuge where we can explore.

Each heartbeat sings of dreams untold,
In this retreat, we break the mold.
Wings unfurl to the softest grace,
In the stillness, we find our space.

Beneath the stars, our visions blend,
In the night, where dreams ascend.
Together, we'll embrace the night,
In depths of dreams, we find our light.

Lullabies of the Hidden Glen

In the glen where shadows play,
Softly sings the end of day.
Moonbeams kiss the emerald grass,
While gentle breezes slowly pass.

Crickets chirp a sweet refrain,
Telling wishes free of pain.
Nature's hush, a lullaby,
Whispers secrets to the sky.

Dancing leaves in twilight's glow,
Guide the dreams that come and go.
From every nook, a tale will start,
Woven deep within the heart.

Sleep now, child of earth and air,
In the glen, you have no care.
Close your eyes and drift away,
In this haven, where hopes sway.

The Network of Whispering Roots

Below the soil, where shadows creep,
A network forms, deep roots that keep.
Branches reach for skies so blue,
While whispers share the tales anew.

In the dark, connections flow,
Silent songs that only they know.
Through the earth, their secrets thread,
Binding life, where all are led.

Each winding root, a story spun,
Of seasons passed and battles won.
Intertwined beneath the ground,
Life's resilience knows no bound.

Listen close, the whispers call,
In unity, we rise or fall.
Together we will forge our way,
In the embrace of roots that sway.

In Search of the Unseen Haven

In the quiet woods, shadows blend,
Where whispers of dreams and daylight end.
A path obscured by the bramble's kiss,
Yearns for the light of a secret bliss.

Footsteps falter, the heart beats fast,
A glimpse of hope from the fading past.
Through tangled vines and the rustling leaves,
The search for solace, the soul believes.

Each brook's laughter, a guiding song,
Invites the weary to journey along.
In the heart of green, where silence reigns,
Lies the unseen haven, free from chains.

Beneath the stars, the night unfolds,
With stories of comfort, yet untold.
A sanctuary found in the hushed embrace,
In search of peace, we find our place.

The Lost Melody of the Hidden Glade

In softest whispers, the echoes play,
A melody lost on the wind's ballet.
Through rustling grass and swaying trees,
A song of the heart floats with the breeze.

Once bright and clear, the notes have fled,
To shadows and dreams, they quietly tread.
In the glade where sunlight used to dance,
Relics of music still hold their chance.

The brook burbles softly, a tender tune,
Beneath the watchful eye of the moon.
With every breath, remember the sound,
Of the lost melody yearning, unbound.

A call to the wanderer, come find your way,
To the secret glade where memories sway.
With open ears, let the spirit roam,
In the lost melody, you'll find your home.

Echoes Beneath Mossy Stones

Beneath the earth, where shadows dwell,
Lie stories of old, too frail to tell.
Mossy stones keep their secrets tight,
Guarding the dreams of the forgotten night.

Each step reveals a story new,
Of lives once lived and loves so true.
Whispers linger in the cool, damp air,
Echoes of laughter, a lingering prayer.

The ancient roots, they twist and weave,
Tales of the past, too precious to leave.
In every crevice, a memory hides,
Echoes beneath where the moss abides.

In twilight's glow, let silence reign,
Hold close the echoes, remember the pain.
For in these stones, a legacy lies,
A tapestry woven beneath the skies.

Traces of the Lost Expedition

With weary feet, we chart unknown,
Through wild terrain, where seeds are sown.
Traces left by those who came,
In quest of glory, a fleeting fame.

Maps unfurl with ink still fresh,
Guiding the brave through nature's flesh.
In every valley, a story waits,
Of trials faced and fateful dates.

The compass spins with restless heart,
As shadows lengthen, we drift apart.
Lost in the wild, yet spirits soar,
For every step opens a new door.

Upon the hills where the brave once roamed,
We trace their paths, where whispers combed.
The lost expedition lives and breathes,
In nature's arms, the soul believes.

The Sigh of the Enigma

In twilight's embrace, whispers unfold,
Secrets untold, in shadows they mold.
A breath of the night, a fleeting delight,
In the depths of silence, the mysteries ignite.

Veils of the cosmos, shimmer and twirl,
Dreams intertwine, in a mystical whirl.
Lost in the echo, the stars softly sigh,
Each moment a puzzle, as time dances by.

Eyes of the ancients, watch from afar,
Guiding the seekers, like a wandering star.
Within the still waters, reflections take flight,
The enigma unravels, beneath the pale light.

With every heartbeat, the riddle expands,
A labyrinth woven by fate's gentle hands.
In the sigh of the dark, where shadows do blend,
The enigma speaks softly, but never an end.

Corners of the Unknown

In the corners where shadows play,
Whispers of secrets, they softly stray.
Chasing the echoes, through paths so gray,
The unknown beckons, leading the way.

Footsteps on cobblestones, tales they tell,
In the heart of the night, there's magic to smell.
Flickers of lanterns, in corners so deep,
Guarding the stories that shadows will keep.

Veils of uncertainty hang in the air,
A dance of the brave, and those unaware.
In the corners where history's breath is drawn,
Lie the dreams of the night, awaiting the dawn.

Turning and twisting, the paths intertwine,
In corners of unknown, the fates align.
With courage as lanterns, we seek and we roam,
Finding ourselves in the corners, we call home.

Chronicles of the Hidden Realm

In the hidden realm where shadows play,
Chronicles whisper of the night's ballet.
Each star a story, each moonbeam a thread,
In the fabric of dreams where the ancient have fled.

Forgotten whispers float through the air,
The echoes of magic, both mysterious and rare.
Amongst the tall trees, where the wild things dwell,
Lie the tales of the moon, weaving a spell.

Through glades of enchantment, and misty streams,
A journey unfolds in the world of dreams.
With every soft rustle, and breath of the night,
The chronicles awaken, in the pale silver light.

So follow the whispers that beckon your heart,
In the hidden realm, where the wonders impart.
Boundless the magic, as starlight reveals,
The chronicles whisper, and the hidden unveils.

The Weaving of Selkie Dreams

In the gentle tide where dreams intertwine,
Selkie songs echo, through ocean's design.
With soft sandy shores, where the sea meets the land,
The weaving of dreams, by nature's own hand.

Moonlight glistens on the surface so clear,
Fables of selkies, in whispers so near.
Each wave carries tales of love lost at sea,
In the depths of the ocean, where hearts long to be.

With silken embraces from deep waters drawn,
The selkies return with the light of the dawn.
Their laughter like petals, on soft ocean breeze,
Weaving through memories, like whispers of trees.

So listen closely, to the ocean's soft sigh,
For the dreams of the selkies are waiting nearby.
In the embrace of the tide, they dance and they gleam,
In the heart of the waves, lies the weaving of dreams.

Beyond the Shaded Path

Whispers weave through twisted trees,
Sunlight dances with the leaves.
Footsteps soft on earth below,
Secrets linger where shadows grow.

Vines curl gently, time stands still,
Nature's hush, a tranquil thrill.
Each turn brings a hidden view,
Mysteries ripe for me and you.

A stream flows gently, crystal clear,
Voices call, yet none are near.
Lost in thought, we wander wide,
Each moment cherished, hearts collide.

The end awaits, a glimmer bright,
Beyond the shaded path, pure light.
Embrace the journey, let it be,
In this realm, we are truly free.

The Embrace of Quiet Realms

In the stillness where shadows lie,
Breath of nature, a gentle sigh.
Soft petals fall, drift through the air,
Whispers echo, free from despair.

Cotton clouds, and blue above,
In this space, we find our love.
Moments linger, soft and sweet,
Peace enfolds us, pure retreat.

The brook hums low, a lullaby,
Stars peek in, a velvet sky.
Here, the world slows to a pause,
In quiet realms, we find our cause.

With every heartbeat, silence sings,
Nature cradles, sweet, soft wings.
Together we can drift and dream,
In this haven, hope's gleam.

Reflection in the Midnight Brook

Moonlight dances on waters deep,
Here in stillness, secrets sleep.
Haunting echoes, tales unsaid,
Ripples whisper where dreams tread.

Stars are mirrored, a thousand eyes,
Glimmers weave through midnight skies.
Time takes pause, the world retreats,
In this moment, wonder meets.

Softly swaying, shadows play,
Words unspoken drift away.
Each reflection tells a tale,
Carried forth on midnight's veil.

Crickets sing their serenade,
In the dark, our fears unmade.
As we gaze, we both can see,
The brook reflects you and me.

The Heart of the Concealed Sanctuary

Hidden deep, where few can tread,
Lies a space where dreams have fled.
Nature's brush paints every hue,
A sanctuary meant for two.

Winding paths of emerald green,
Whispers secret, softly seen.
Cool shade wraps like a gentle hug,
In this realm, our souls can snug.

The wind carries a gentle song,
In this place, we both belong.
Time unwinds in a sacred flow,
Each heartbeat feels the garden grow.

Together here, the world feels right,
In the heart of soft glowing light.
Let us linger, hearts entwined,
In this sanctuary, love defined.

Echoes of the Shrouded Meadow

In whispers soft, the shadows play,
The meadow dreams, where sunbeams sway.
Beneath the sky, in colors bright,
The echoes dance, a fleeting light.

Moonlit paths through grass so green,
Where laughter lingers, yet unseen.
With every step, a secret calls,
In shrouded hues, where spirit thralls.

The breeze tells tales of days gone by,
Of fleeting moments, shadows nigh.
In twilight's arms, the silence sings,
Of magic held in simple things.

So tread with care on twilight's floor,
Where echoes linger, forevermore.
Each blade of grass, a story spun,
In the shrouded meadow, we are one.

Mysteries of the Forgotten Canyon

Deep in the earth, the whispers creep,
Through rugged walls, the shadows leap.
Ancient stones guard tales untold,
Of silent journeys, brave and bold.

Winding paths through canyon wide,
Beneath the stars, where dreams abide.
Each crack and crevice, stories share,
Of fleeting echoes caught in air.

A river's song, a lover's call,
The forgotten canyon holds them all.
Where time stands still and night unfolds,
In mysteries wrapped, the heart beholds.

So wander deep, let secrets flow,
In hidden depths, where wonders grow.
The canyon waits, both fierce and grand,
For those who seek, and understand.

Shadows Among the Ferns

In emerald hues, the ferns do sway,
Where shadows linger, and spirits play.
The forest whispers, soft and low,
In the gentle dance of winds that blow.

Secrets hide in leafy green,
Where flighty dreams in silence glean.
Each shadow casts a story bright,
In daylight's grace or velvet night.

Among the ferns, the heart finds peace,
In nature's arms, a sweet release.
As twilight falls, the world grows still,
In shadows deep, where time can't kill.

So walk among these whispered leaves,
And find the truths that nature weaves.
In the hidden realms, let spirits dance,
Through shadows soft, in a timeless trance.

Lost in the Veiled Woods

In veils of mist, the woods do sigh,
Where lost souls wander, and memories fly.
Each twisted path leads dreams astray,
In hidden realms where shadows play.

The trees stand tall, guardians wise,
Beneath the watchful, ancient skies.
With every rustle, whispers call,
Of fleeting moments, great and small.

Among the thickets, secrets bloom,
With every footfall, dispelling gloom.
A canvas painted in dusk's embrace,
In the veiled woods, we find our place.

So lose yourself in nature bold,
In stories shared, forever told.
Through winding trails, let spirits roam,
In the veiled woods, we find a home.

Murmurs from the Enshrouded Woods

Whispers dance among the trees,
Secrets linger in the breeze.
Shadows weave in twilight's grace,
Nature's heart, a hidden place.

Moonlight spills on forest floor,
Echoes call from ancient lore.
Footfalls soft on emerald bed,
Mysteries where few have tread.

Leaves caress with gentle sighs,
Starlit paths and lullabies.
In the hush, the wild things speak,
Silence grows; it's solace we seek.

Night unveils its velvet veil,
Murmurs weave a timeless tale.
In the dark, the woods remain,
Secrets held within their brain.

Footprints on the Forgotten Trail

Steps once marked in dusty earth,
Whispers echo of their worth.
Through the thickets, quietly tread,
Stories linger of those who led.

Time has claimed this winding way,
Nature's grip will not betray.
Branches arch in solemn keep,
Sowing dreams where shadows creep.

Each footprint speaks of distant days,
Adventures sung in sunlit rays.
Lost but not forgotten, they
Guide the heart that dares to stray.

Through the overgrowth, we roam,
In this maze, we find our home.
Paths may vanish, yet we find
That the journey shapes the mind.

Blooming in the Twilight Glade

Petals open in soft twilight,
Colors shimmer with fading light.
Fragrant blooms in twilight's breath,
Dance away the day's slow death.

Silent songs of night begin,
As the stars awake within.
Dewdrops glisten, jewels rare,
Nature's beauty beyond compare.

In the shadows, whispers sigh,
Butterflies like dreams drift by.
In this glade where magic stirs,
Hearts entwined, as silence purrs.

Each moment holds the softest grace,
As twilight paints the sky's embrace.
Blooming dreams of love's sweet fate,
In the glade, we celebrate.

Harmony of the Cloistered Oasis

In the heart of dunes, a blessing,
Whispers cool, the winds caressing.
Water flows with tranquil song,
Peaceful haven, where we belong.

Palms sway gently, a soft lull,
Nature's touch, forever null.
In sunlight's dance on crystal ground,
Harmony in silence found.

Lotus blooms, a sacred sight,
Night awakens, stars ignite.
Every sound, a tender grace,
In this tranquil, sacred space.

As moonlight drapes the lush retreat,
Hearts gather, feel the pulse, complete.
In the oasis, love will gleam,
In every whisper, every dream.

The Hidden Harbor of Time

In whispers soft, the waters tread,
A harbor waits with secrets dead.
The moonlight dances on the wave,
While shadows linger, silent, brave.

Time's vessel hides in twilight's hold,
Where echoes linger, tales unfold.
A gentle breeze, the sails are drawn,
To drift away with quiet dawn.

Here moments blend, a fleeting rhyme,
In distant lands, the sands of time.
With each heartbeat, the clock unwinds,
In hidden nooks, the past unwinds.

The harbor calls to souls adrift,
With every wave, a subtle gift.
In stillness found, the world retreats,
As time unveils its tender beats.

Beneath the Cloak of Verdant Dreams

In leafy shades, where whispers weave,
A world awakens, hearts believe.
The emerald cloak, a soft embrace,
In dreams we find our sacred space.

Amidst the ferns, a path unknown,
Where secrets of the heart are shown.
The sunbeams dance on dewy ground,
In nature's song, true peace is found.

The gentle breeze brings tales anew,
Of creatures small and skies so blue.
With every rustle, life's refrain,
In verdant dreams, we set our gain.

Beneath the cloak, the senses bloom,
In tranquil shade, we find our room.
As roots entwine, the soul takes flight,
In dreams so green, we greet the light.

The Place Where Time Pauses

In shadows cast by ancient trees,
Time clings lightly to the breeze.
Each moment rests, a breath, a sigh,
As whispers linger, soft and high.

A quiet nook, where worries fade,
In sunlight's warmth, the fear will wade.
Here memories fold like gentle sheets,
And every pulse of life repeats.

The stillness blooms like flowers rare,
Inviting peace, a tender care.
In the embrace of timeless grace,
We find our rhythm, our true place.

Where seconds pause, and hearts align,
In tranquil depths, sweet souls entwine.
Each heartbeat sings a serenade,
In this still realm, our fears evade.

Harmony in the Camouflaged Nook

In tangled vines, a haven hides,
Where nature's chorus softly glides.
Amongst the leaves, life intertwines,
In hidden nooks, a song defines.

The rustling paths of secret trails,
Where every step the heartbeat hails.
With hues of green and golden glint,
In camouflaged peace, our lives imprint.

A crevice found, with shelter deep,
Where dreams awaken from their sleep.
In harmony, the world unfolds,
As silent stories dare be told.

The rhythm flows like murmured streams,
In whispered thoughts, we weave our dreams.
In a nook where quiet reigns supreme,
We find the essence of our theme.

A Tread Amongst Secret Ferns

In a forest deep and green,
The ferns sway low, unseen.
A path unfolds, soft beneath,
Whispers dance with every breath.

Glimmers caught in morning dew,
Nature's art in shades of hue.
Step by step, the heart ignites,
As silence plays with dusky lights.

Sunlight filters through the leaves,
Each shadow bends, each moment weaves.
Ferns embrace the gentle tread,
Secrets held like dreams unsaid.

The world beyond fades from view,
In this realm, a soul renews.
A tread amongst the ferns of old,
A story whispered, softly told.

The Cloak of Nature's Whispers

Underneath the starry sky,
Nature's whispers drift and sigh.
A cloak of night wraps close with care,
Secrets linger in the air.

Leaves rustle soft like lover's breath,
In shadows deep, there lies a depth.
Every pause, a gentle song,
A place where all the heart belongs.

Moonlight spills on emerald grass,
Time slows down as echoes pass.
The stars above, they wink and sway,
In nature's cloak, we lose our way.

Wrapped in warmth of twilight's kiss,
Moments shared, a fleeting bliss.
Beneath this vast celestial dome,
The whispers weave us safely home.

Secrets in the Moonlit Meadow

In the meadow's hush and glow,
Secrets wait where moonbeams flow.
Whispers carried on the breeze,
Every shadow bends with ease.

Flowers bloom with silver light,
The world is draped in soft delight.
Listen close to stories old,
In the night, their magic unfolds.

Grasses sway with gentle grace,
Each petal holds a hidden place.
Mysteries dance in soft embrace,
In this tranquil, sacred space.

A stroll beneath the watchful stars,
Where silence speaks, and nothing mars.
Secrets linger, soft and low,
In the meadow's moonlit glow.

Dancing Shadows of the Unseen

In the twilight deep and wide,
Dancing shadows start to glide.
Figures weave through night's facade,
The unseen play, a hushed charade.

Footsteps echo with a thrill,
In the dark, the air stands still.
Every flicker, every sway,
Holds stories longing to convey.

Mysteries swirl like autumn leaves,
In a dance where no one grieves.
The silent steps speak in dreams,
Where nothing's ever as it seems.

In the dark, stars watch and gleam,
Shadows moving like a dream.
Through the void, they slyly weave,
Dancing shadows, hearts believe.

Beneath the Whispering Boughs

Underneath the ancient trees,
The sunlight dances in the leaves.
Whispers echo with the breeze,
Nature's secrets softly weave.

Creatures stir in dappled shade,
Hidden paths twist and entwine.
Every step, a gentle raid,
On the stories, time defines.

With every rustle, dreams take flight,
In the calm of twilight's glow.
Beneath the boughs, hearts feel light,
And the world outside moves slow.

Here beneath the whispering trees,
Magic lingers in the air.
With each sigh, the spirit frees,
In this haven, pure and rare.

Mists of the Enchanted Dell

In the dell where shadows play,
Mists rise softly from the ground.
Whispers of the night, they sway,
In this realm, enchantments found.

Ferns unfurl like emerald fans,
Moonlight bathes the hidden brook.
Mysteries flow like fine grains of sand,
In the pages of a forgotten book.

Crisp and cool, the dew-kissed air,
Holds the dreams of fae and sprite.
Each breath drawn, a lover's prayer,
In the soft embrace of night.

Here, where time stands still and hushed,
Hearts awaken to the call.
Lost in fantasies, we're brushed,
By the magic of it all.

Guardians of the Overgrown Path

Tall and proud, the sentinels rise,
Through the thick of tangled green.
With steadfast watch, they claim the skies,
Guardians where the wilds have been.

Vines drape low, a curtain dense,
As footsteps fade upon the trail.
Every turn holds tales immense,
In the hush where echoes sail.

Birds take flight, against the shade,
A symphony of nature's hymn.
Through the growth, old dreams cascade,
In the light that starts to dim.

Here we wander, lost but found,
Among the whispers of the past.
In this sacred, magic ground,
Time stands still, forever cast.

Reflections in the Quiet Waters

Serene and calm, the waters lie,
Mirroring the twilight's glow.
Ripples dance as stars pass by,
Ripened dreams begin to flow.

Silhouettes in muted tones,
Ghostly figures step and fade.
Every splash, a soft sweet moan,
In the depths, secrets are laid.

Here the world is calm and pure,
Thoughts drift like leaves on the stream.
In this peace, hearts find their cure,
Lost in echoes of a dream.

Reflections speak of love and loss,
Glimmers of a timeless grace.
In this realm, we bear our cross,
Finding solace in the space.

Vows of the Hidden Orchard

Beneath the boughs, a secret grows,
Whispers of love in petals close.
Silent promises in the air,
Nature's vows, a bond so rare.

The fruits of patience, ripe and sweet,
Each tender heartbeat, a rhythmic beat.
In sunlight's glow, shadows play,
In this orchard, hearts will stay.

Rustling leaves in summer's heat,
Echoing secrets where lovers meet.
The gentle breeze, a soft caress,
In hidden corners, we find our rest.

Together we weave, hand in hand,
In the silence, we softly stand.
Under the stars, our dreams take flight,
In this orchard, love feels right.

Solstice Serenade in the Concealed Ridge

On the ridge where shadows blend,
A melody of time we send.
The sun dips low, a golden spark,
With every note, we greet the dark.

Whispers rise with twilight's loom,
Nature hums a timeless tune.
In this hour, the world feels wide,
As secrets dance in the evening tide.

Stars awaken, bright and clear,
In this serenade, you are near.
The earth turns slow, as if to see,
Our laughter mingles with the trees.

The solstice breathes a gentle sigh,
As shadows stretch across the sky.
With every heartbeat, life in tune,
In the concealed ridge, love is our boon.

Whispers in the Hidden Glen

In the glen where time stands still,
Whispers flow like a gentle thrill.
Cascading dreams among the trees,
Nature's breath, a lullaby breeze.

Each leaf a secret, soft and low,
In hidden paths, our spirits go.
Beneath the boughs, we find our way,
In silent moments that softly sway.

Sunbeams filter through leafy veils,
In this glen, our love prevails.
Every rustle tells a tale,
In this sacred place, we sail.

Through tender sighs, hearts align,
In whispers warm, your hand in mine.
Forever cherished, our souls entwined,
In the hidden glen, peace we find.

The Enchanted Hollow

In the hollow where magic dwells,
A world of wonder, secrets tell.
Mossy carpets beneath our feet,
Each corner holds a heartbeat sweet.

Glowing fireflies dance at dusk,
In this place, life's gentle husk.
A symphony of nature's art,
Whispered spells that fill the heart.

Overhead, the canopy sighs,
Beneath its embrace, no goodbyes.
In every shadow, dreams take flight,
In this hollow, everything feels right.

In the twilight, we gently sway,
With love as our guide, we find our way.
Together we roam where the wild things grow,
In the enchanted hollow, our spirits glow.

Reveries in the Masked Wilderness

In shadows deep, where whispers play,
The winds weave tales, both night and day.
Beneath the boughs of ancient trees,
Dreams dance lightly on the breeze.

A hidden brook sings soft and low,
As stars above begin to glow.
Through tangled roots, the heart finds peace,
In nature's arms, all troubles cease.

The moon unveils a silver grace,
Casting light upon each face.
A journey starts where silence calls,
In the wild's embrace, the spirit sprawls.

Forgotten paths yet to explore,
In reveries, our spirits soar.
The masked wilderness holds its key,
To open doors for you and me.

Forgotten Paths of the Lush Haven

Veiled in green, the pathways fade,
Where stories linger, memories laid.
Among the trees, so tall and wise,
Echoes whisper through the skies.

Lush havens call with gentle sighs,
Dew-kissed petals in sunrise.
Each step taken, a soft embrace,
Nature's rhythm, a sacred space.

Through tangled vines and flowers bright,
Lost in time, where shadows light.
With every turn, the heart ignites,
On forgotten paths, pure delight.

As sunlight weaves through leafy veil,
A tale unfolds, a whispered trail.
In this haven, we find our way,
In nature's arms, forever stay.

The Veil of Time's Tapestry

Threads of ages intertwine,
In the fabric where dreams align.
A tapestry spun of joy and strife,
Holding echoes of past life.

Moments captured, stitched with care,
Lost in time, they linger there.
Each color a memory, vibrant and bold,
As the stories of old are gently told.

Beneath the veil, forgotten fates,
A dance of shadows, time awaits.
In the stillness, the heart can see,
The beauty of what used to be.

As we traverse this sacred quilt,
Woven memories, gently built.
In the veil of time, we find our place,
In every thread, a soft embrace.

Glimpses of the Obscured Retreat

In secret woods where silence reigns,
Glimpses of peace break the chains.
Amid the leaves, a soft voice calls,
To hidden nooks where nature falls.

The sun breaks through with tender rays,
Illuminating forgotten days.
Here, time bends, and worries cease,
In the obscured retreat, find your peace.

Waves of green in a lush embrace,
Every rustle, a gentle grace.
As butterflies spin a tale of light,
We drift in dreams, in pure delight.

Once lost in the world's frenetic grind,
In this haven, solace we find.
In glimpses bright, the heart takes flight,
In the obscured retreat, pure delight.

Milton Keynes UK
Ingram Content Group UK Ltd.
UKHW022050111124
451035UK00014B/1039